Ellis Island

Elizabeth Carney

NATIONAL
GEOGRAPHIC

Washington, D.C.

To all the immigrants who bravely took a chance to secure a better life for future generations. Especially my namesake, Elizabeth Bardar, who passed through Ellis Island in 1920. —E. A. C.

Published by National Geographic Partners, LLC, Washington, D.C. 20036.

Library of Congress
Cataloging-in-Publication Data

Carney, Elizabeth, 1981-
  Ellis island / by Elizabeth Carney.
    pages cm. — (National geographic kids readers)
  Includes index.
  ISBN 978-1-4263-2341-6 (pbk. : alk. paper) — ISBN 978-1-4263-2342-3 (library binding : alk. paper)
  1. Ellis Island Immigration Station (N.Y. and N.J.) 2. United States—Emigration and immigration. I. Title.
  JV6484.C37 2016
  304.8'73—dc23
                                        2015028054

Art Director: Amanda Larsen
Designer: YAY! Design

The publisher and author gratefully acknowledge the expert content review of this book by Vincent Cannato, associate professor, History Department, University of Massachusetts Boston, and the literacy review of this book by Mariam Jean Dreher, professor of reading education, University of Maryland, College Park.

Photo Credits

Cover, Lewis W. Hine/New York Public Library; 1, Masterfile; 3 (LORT), Shutterstock; 4, Gallo Images/Getty Images; 5, The Granger Collection, New York; 6, Nikreates/Alamy; 9 (CTR), Rue des Archives/The Granger Collection; 9 (UPLE), AG-PHOTOS/Shutterstock; 11 (UP), Print Collector/Getty Images; 12 (LOLE), s_oleg/Shutterstock; 12 (LORT), Yellowj/Shutterstock; 13 (UP), The New York Public Library; 13 (LO), Corbis; 14-15, The New York Public Library; 16-17, J. Irwin/Fotosearch; 18, Photo Researchers/Getty Images; 19, Commission of Immigration (Ellis Island, N.Y.)/National Geographic Creative; 20, International Museum of Photography at George Eastman/National Geographic Creative; 21 (LO CTR), The Granger Collection, New York/The Granger Collection; 21 (LORT), Jennifer Booher/Alamy; 22, The New York Public Library; 23, The Granger Collection; 24 (UP), Blend Images/Getty Images; 24 (CTR), Joseph Sohm/Shutterstock; 24 (LO), Underwood Archives/Getty Images; 25 (UP), Viacheslav Lopatin/Shutterstock; 25 (CTR), The Granger Collection; 25 (LO), ullstein bild/Getty Images; 26, The Granger Collection; 27 (UP), The Granger Collection; 27 (LO CTR), The Granger Collection; 28, Library of Congress Prints and Photographs Division; 29, Hemis/Alamy; 30, The Granger Collection; 31 (UP), The Granger Collection; 31 (LORT), Courtesy of the Ellis Island National Museum of Immigration; 32, The New York Public Library; 33, Gamma-Keystone/Getty Images; 34, The Granger Collection; 35 (ALL), The Granger Collection; 36 (CTR), Roger Viollet/Getty Images; 36 (LOLE), The LIFE Picture Collection/Getty Images; 37 (LE), NY Daily News/Getty Images; 37 (RT), ullstein bild/Getty Images; 39 (ALL), The Granger Collection; 40 (UP), Stephen Wilkes/National Geographic Creative; 40 (LO), National Park Service/National Geographic Creative; 41, Carol M. Highsmith Archive/Library of Congress Prints and Photographs Division; 42-43, Atlantide Phototravel/Corbis; 42 (UPLE), AXL/Shutterstock; 44 (UP), Gallo Images/Getty Images; 44 (CTR), Hulton Archive/Getty Images; 44 (LO), The Granger Collection; 45 (UP), Lewis W. Hine/George Eastman House/Getty Images; 45 (LORT), iofoto/Shutterstock; 45 (CTR LE), Naughty-Nut/Shutterstock; 45 (LO CTR), Gabrielle Hovey/Shutterstock; 45 (CTR RT), Eyewire; 45 (UP CTR), Orhan Cam/Shutterstock; 45 (CTR RT), Corbis; 46 (UP), The New York Public Library; 46 (CTR LE), The Granger Collection; 46 (CTR RT), The Granger Collection; 46 (LOLE), Atlantide Phototravel/Corbis; 46 (LORT), Library of Congress Prints and Photographs Division; 47 (UPLE), The Granger Collection; 47 (UPRT), Library of Congress Prints and Photographs Division; 47 (CTR LE), The Granger Collection; 47 (CTR RT), Rue des Archives/The Granger Collection; 47 (LOLE), Print Collector/Getty Images; 47 (LORT), The Granger Collection; vocab (THROUGHOUT), Chamille White/Shutterstock; header (THROUGHOUT), nazlisart/Shutterstock

National Geographic supports K–12 educators with ELA Common Core Resources. Visit natgeoed.org/commoncore for more information.

Printed in the United States of America
16/WOR/1

Table of Contents

Island of Hope   4

American Dreams   8

A Difficult Trip   10

Gull Island   12

Buildings of Ellis Island   16

On American Soil   18

6 Cool Facts About Ellis Island   24

Trouble Upon Arrival   26

Helping Out   30

Beyond Ellis Island   32

Making an Impact   34

A Deserted Village   38

Restoring a Monument   40

Quiz Whiz   44

Glossary   46

Index   48

Island of Hope

It was New Year's Day in 1892. Annie Moore took her two little brothers' hands. They walked onto the dock at Ellis Island, New York. A government building on the island had just opened. There, workers would decide whether to let them into the United States.

The main building on Ellis Island, as it looks today

Immigrants arriving on Ellis Island, around 1900

Annie and her brothers were immigrants. They had come from another country and were looking for a new life in America. Annie would be the first to walk through the building's doors. Over the next 30 years, millions would follow.

Words to Know

IMMIGRANT: Someone who comes to a country to live there permanently

This statue of Annie Moore and her brothers stands in Cobh, Ireland.

Seventeen-year-old Annie had sailed across the Atlantic Ocean from her home in Ireland. She and her brothers made the trip alone. Their parents had moved to New York City two years earlier. They had saved up the money to pay for their children's trip.

Officials looked over the kids and said Annie and her brothers could enter America. Because Annie was the first immigrant to arrive at Ellis Island, one official gave her a $10 gold piece. It was the most money Annie had ever had.

Words to Know

OFFICIAL: A person who is elected or given a specific job, often involving work for the government

American Dreams

From 1892 to 1924, Ellis Island served as the main gateway to America. As each steamship chugged into New York Harbor, immigrants saw the Statue of Liberty. To them, the statue stood for the freedom they wanted so badly.

In the late 1800s and early 1900s, life in Europe was very difficult. Many people were forced to leave their homelands. In some places, you could be jailed or killed for practicing a certain religion or speaking out against the government. Food and jobs were hard to find. Many immigrants believed that America offered the best chance for a better life.

Words to Know

STEAMSHIP: A ship powered by steam engines

In Her Own Words

"We saw the Statue of Liberty and Mother said to me, 'That means we are free.'"
—Margaret Wertle, arrived from Hungary at age seven

Immigrants arrive in New York Harbor and see the Statue of Liberty in the early 1900s.

A Difficult Trip

Immigrants from Europe had to cross the Atlantic Ocean to reach America. During Ellis Island's busiest years, immigrants came on steamships. The voyage lasted about 12 days.

Most steamship passengers traveled in steerage. These tickets were the cheapest. But in steerage, it was uncomfortable and dangerous. No fresh air reached this part of the ship. Hundreds of people packed into crowded bunks. The vomit of seasick passengers covered the floor. Most immigrants couldn't wait to arrive in America and get off the ship!

Words to Know

STEERAGE: The bottom section of the ship, where passengers paying the cheapest fare traveled

This drawing shows steerage passengers on their way to America.

Arctic Ocean

NORTH AMERICA

United States

Ellis Island

59%

33%

6%

EUROPE

ASIA

Atlantic Ocean

AFRICA

ASIA

Pacific Ocean

Indian Ocean

AUSTRALIA

SOUTH AMERICA

Where Ellis Island Immigrants Came From

Northern and Western Europe

Eastern and Southern Europe

South America, Central America, and the Caribbean

Asia

0   2000 miles

0   2000 kilometers

ANTARCTICA

While most immigrants from Asia entered the United States on the West Coast, a few did come through Ellis Island. The percentages of people from different areas of the world are rounded. That is why the total sum of the percentages does not equal 100 percent.

Gull Island

Immigrants may not have known it, but the little island they were arriving on had a long history. Hundreds of years ago, the island barely peeked above the water during high tides. The Lenape Native Americans called it Kioshk, which means gull island. Only seagulls lived there.

In 1624, the Dutch arrived at what is now called New York City. They called the little island Little Oyster Island for the oysters they harvested from its shores.

Oysters

Seagull

An illustration of the Dutch buying Manhattan Island, New York, from the Lenape Native Americans in 1626

One of the earliest paintings of New York Harbor

A drawing from 1820 shows lower Manhattan Island and the types of boats used at the time.

Many years later, New York became a British colony. In 1774, right before the Revolutionary War, an American businessman named Samuel Ellis bought the little island. Ellis named the island after himself.

Words to Know

COLONY: An area controlled by people living in another country. New York was one of the 13 American Colonies controlled by the British.

REVOLUTIONARY WAR: The war between the American Colonies and the British during 1775–1783. The Colonies wanted to be free from British control.

INSPECTED: Looked over carefully

The U.S. government took over Ellis Island in 1808 and built a small fort. After that, the island was used mainly to store gunpowder.

It wasn't until 1890 that officials decided to build an immigration station on Ellis Island. Some people thought it was best to keep immigrants off the mainland while they were inspected. Then they could enter America.

That's a FACT! In the late 1800s, workers dumped tons of dirt and rock from subway tunnels onto Ellis Island to make it bigger.

Buildings of Ellis Island

CAFETERIA: Ellis Island cooks prepared and served meals for immigrants while they waited on the island.

BAGGAGE AND DORMITORY: Some immigrants didn't get permission to enter the United States right away. They had to drop off their bags and head to dormitories, where many slept in bunk beds.

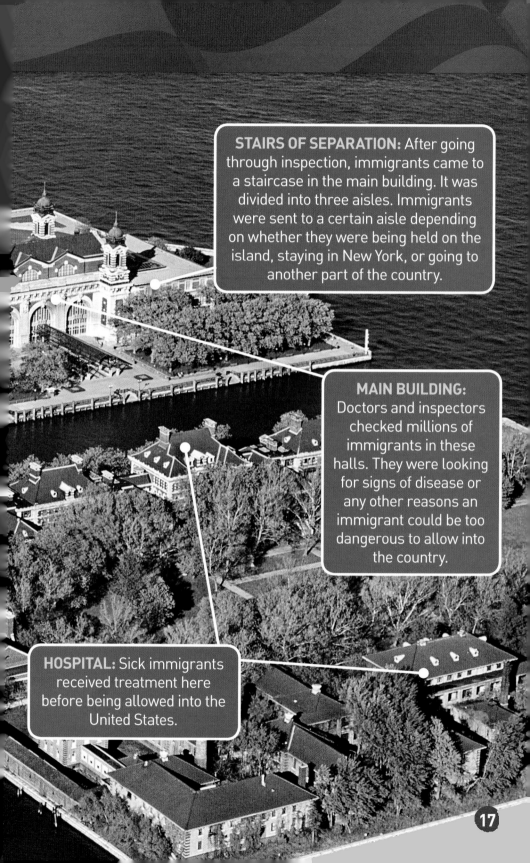

STAIRS OF SEPARATION: After going through inspection, immigrants came to a staircase in the main building. It was divided into three aisles. Immigrants were sent to a certain aisle depending on whether they were being held on the island, staying in New York, or going to another part of the country.

MAIN BUILDING: Doctors and inspectors checked millions of immigrants in these halls. They were looking for signs of disease or any other reasons an immigrant could be too dangerous to allow into the country.

HOSPITAL: Sick immigrants received treatment here before being allowed into the United States.

On American Soil

Immigrants carrying their belongings

Imagine it: You arrive in a new country after a hard trip. You have little more than the money in your pockets and a few of your most precious things. People wearing uniforms poke you, inspect you, and ask you questions. It's like taking a difficult test that you just hope to pass.

Most passengers had to wait a long time during the immigration process at Ellis Island. At best, they were allowed to enter the United States. At worst, they were sent back to the countries from which they came.

An immigrant Hungarian family

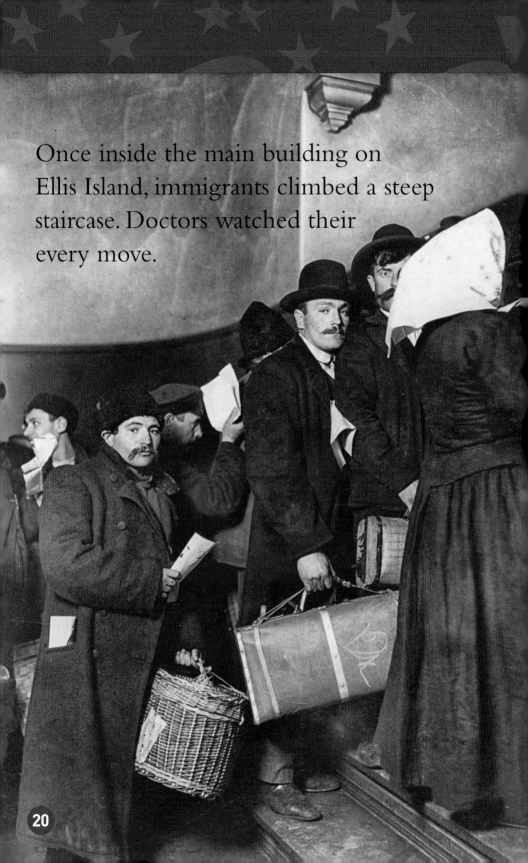

Once inside the main building on Ellis Island, immigrants climbed a steep staircase. Doctors watched their every move.

If people appeared sick or disabled, they were pulled away from their families and given a full medical exam.

The Dreaded Buttonhook

Doctors checked immigrants for an infection that causes blindness. It was common in Europe but not in the United States. The doctors turned the immigrants' eyelids inside out with a tool called a buttonhook. People who showed signs of infection were sent back to their home countries.

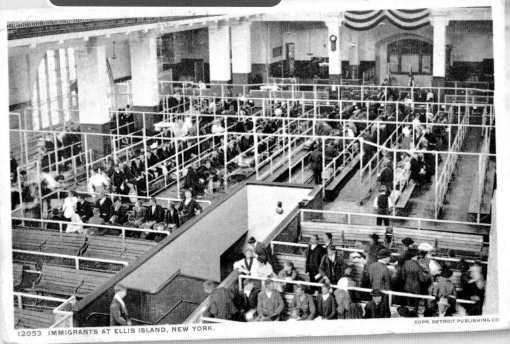

The Registry Room on Ellis Island

12053 IMMIGRANTS AT ELLIS ISLAND, NEW YORK.

COPR. DETROIT PUBLISHING CO.

The next stop was the huge Registry Room. Here people waited to answer questions from other inspectors. Interpreters reworded the inspectors' questions into the immigrants' home languages.

Words to Know

INTERPRETER: A person who puts words in one language into another language

Inspectors asked, "How old are you?" "Are you married?" "What's your job or trade?" They wanted to make sure the immigrants' answers matched the information in the ships' records. They also asked questions about right and wrong behavior. They hoped to spot likely criminals.

This inspection took only a few minutes. Most immigrants passed. The reward? A landing card that officially allowed them to enter the United States.

6 COOL FACTS About Ellis Island

More than 40 percent of Americans today can trace their roots back to one or more people who came through Ellis Island.

1

During its busiest years, Ellis Island had 5,000 immigrants pass through it per day.

2

Fiorello La Guardia worked as an interpreter on Ellis Island for three years. He later served as a U.S. congressman and then as mayor of New York City.

3

4

More Ellis Island immigrants came from Italy than from any other country.

Colosseum in Rome, Italy

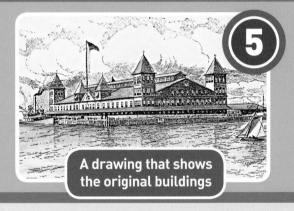

5

A drawing that shows the original buildings

Made completely of wood, the original Ellis Island buildings caught fire in June 1897. They burned to the ground in six hours. The current buildings opened on December 17, 1900.

Less than 2 percent of the 12 million people who passed through Ellis Island's doors failed inspection. They were sent back to their home countries.

6

Trouble Upon Arrival

What happened when immigrants didn't pass inspection right away? Sick immigrants went to the island's hospital for care. Sometimes, people who didn't pass the first round of questions were held for more questioning.

Women traveling alone were not allowed to leave Ellis Island until a relative came to meet them.

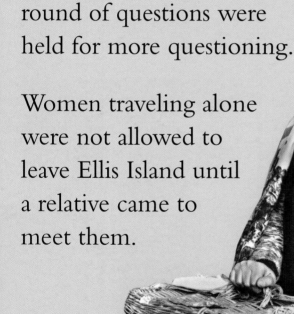

An immigrant woman waits at Ellis Island.

A dormitory for women and children at Ellis Island

This photo shows a dining hall in 1907. These immigrants were waiting to be allowed entrance into America.

This fenced area on the roof of the main building held immigrants who were being deported.

After a while, officials allowed most immigrants into America. But a small number ended up being deported. Usually such people didn't have enough money to try to move to America again. For them, their dreams of living in America were over.

Name Changes

Many people believe that inspectors changed their family's last name when their ancestors arrived at Ellis Island. But that didn't happen. Instead, the inspectors at Ellis Island were most concerned about making sure immigrants' names matched ship records—they didn't care about spellings. The inspectors worked closely with interpreters, who spoke an average of six languages. Interpreters tried to make sure there were no misunderstandings between inspectors and immigrants.

So why did some name changes happen? It was common for immigrants to change their names themselves after arriving in the U.S. They often did this to make their names sound more American or to fit in with the local community.

People search for names of family members at the American Immigrant Wall of Honor on Ellis Island.

Helping Out

Groups of people often helped Ellis Island immigrants in need. They brought warm clothes, food, music, and treats, especially for the children.

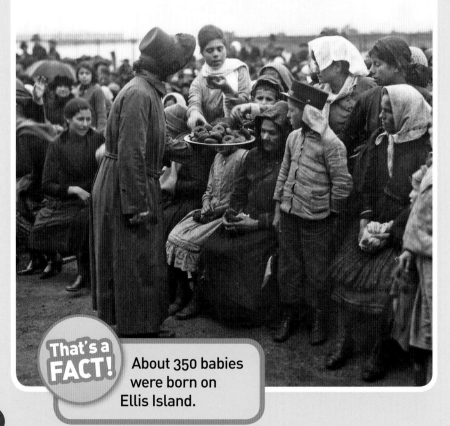

A volunteer gives doughnuts to immigrants at Ellis Island in 1920.

That's a FACT!

About 350 babies were born on Ellis Island.

Immigrant children played on the rooftop garden.

One of the best known helpers was Ludmila Kuchar Foxlee. She immigrated to the United States when she was four. She knew what the immigrants were going through. Foxlee kept detailed records and worked with a large number of immigrants. She organized holiday parties and other festivals to cheer up immigrants held on the island.

Ludmila Kuchar Foxlee

Beyond Ellis Island

Immigrants' experiences on Ellis Island were only the beginning. Landing cards in hand, they set out to begin their lives in America. Some immigrants stayed in New York City. Many traveled to places where they had family and friends who had immigrated earlier. They looked for jobs and places to live.

A photo from 1900 showing immigrants in Manhattan, New York

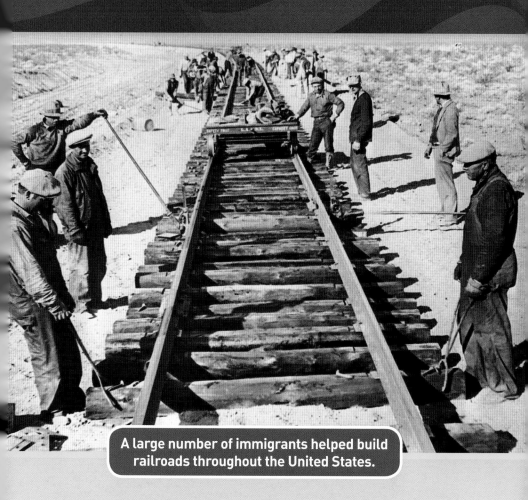

A large number of immigrants helped build railroads throughout the United States.

Many immigrants flocked to parts of the country that were growing. Sometimes immigrants filled entire communities. Common jobs for immigrants included working at mills or factories, working as loggers, or building railroads.

Making an Impact

The United States would be a very different place without immigrants. From food to music to sports, immigrants have shaped the American way of life. As immigrants poured into the country through Ellis Island and other immigration centers, America became known as a "melting pot." This means that America was a place where cultures mixed freely.

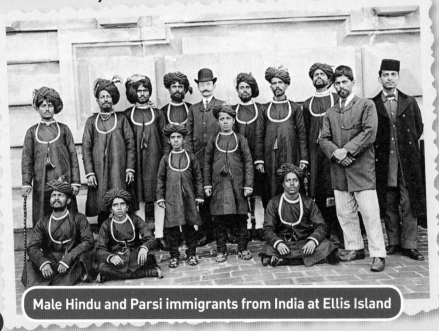

Male Hindu and Parsi immigrants from India at Ellis Island

Immigrants from Ukraine or Russia

A Jewish immigrant from Armenia

A family from Germany

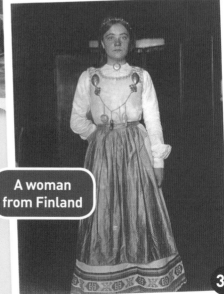

A woman from Finland

Words to Know

CULTURE: The beliefs, traditions, art, and language of a group of people at a certain place and time

35

Meet a few of the immigrants who passed through Ellis Island. They—and many others—went on to accomplish great things.

CLAUDETTE COLBERT was a Broadway actress and film star. When she was eight, she and her family moved from France to New York, coming through Ellis Island in 1911.

Songwriter **IRVING BERLIN** came to the United States through Ellis Island in 1893. He went on to write "God Bless America" and many other popular songs.

HARRY HOUDINI immigrated to the United States from Hungary in 1878. Houdini became a world-famous magician and stuntman. He passed through Ellis Island in 1914 after performing magic shows in Europe. He was a U.S. citizen by that time, but the island still served as the entry point for most people arriving in New York by ship.

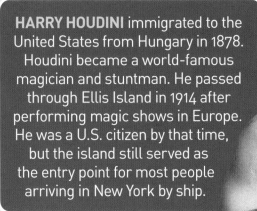

ABRAHAM BEAME was a baby when his family came through Ellis Island in 1906. They came from London to join Beame's father in New York City. Beame later served as the city's mayor from 1974 to 1977.

A Deserted Village

In the 1920s, the United States passed laws that limited the number of immigrants who were allowed into the country. Fewer and fewer people passed through the once-busy island. One worker at the time compared the island to a deserted village.

In the 1940s, the U.S. government used the island for a different purpose. It became a prison to hold people accused of siding with America's enemies during World War II.

After the war, only a few dozen immigrants came through Ellis Island each year. Ellis Island closed for good in 1954.

A man in his sleeping quarters; he was held at Ellis Island around 1943.

A view of the recreation fields on Ellis Island around 1943

Restoring a Monument

This room was used as a hospital ward. Below is what it looked like when it was in use. Above is how the room looked before it was restored.

Once Ellis Island shut down, its buildings fell to ruin. President Lyndon Johnson named Ellis Island a national monument in 1965. But no money was spent on fixing it up.

Finally, in the 1980s, a group called the Statue of Liberty–Ellis Island Foundation worked to raise money to restore the site. The work cost $160 million. At the time, the project was the most expensive of its kind. When the main building was finished, it looked similar to the way it did long ago.

Words to Know

RESTORE: To repair something to bring it back to its original condition

In His Own Words

"I wanted to be an American. I wanted to make the most of my opportunities. And I did just that."
—Charles Beller, arrived from Russia at age six

On September 10, 1990, Ellis Island opened as a museum. Today, more than two million people visit each year. The exhibits tell the story of U.S. immigration. Some people go to learn more about when their ancestors came to America.

In these halls, visitors learn about the brave people who risked so much for a chance at a better life. They began their journey as immigrants. In time, they called themselves Americans.

A view of the main building on Ellis Island today

QUIZ WHIZ

How much do you know about Ellis Island? After reading this book, probably a lot! Take this quiz and find out.

Answers are at the bottom of page 45.

1

Ellis Island is now a _____ .

A. museum
B. port
C. library
D. train station

2

Why did most steamship passengers travel in steerage?

A. It was cheapest.
B. It was luxurious.
C. It was safest.
D. It was fastest.

More Ellis Island immigrants came from _____ than from any other country.

A. Russia
B. Ireland
C. Germany
D. Italy

3

4

Which of the following describes the job of an interpreter?

A. cook and serve food
B. put words in one language into another language
C. perform eye inspections
D. decide which immigrants can enter a country

5

What happened to immigrants who were deported?

A. They were put in jail.
B. They were transported to New York City.
C. They were given a landing card.
D. They were sent back to their home countries.

6

Ellis Island is located near what other national monument?

A. the White House
B. the Statue of Liberty
C. Fort Sumter
D. Mount Rushmore

Which of the following was NOT a use for Ellis Island at one time or another?

A. prison
B. immigration station
C. courthouse
D. fort

7

Answers: 1. A, 2. A, 3. D, 4. B, 5. D, 6. B, 7. C

Glossary

COLONY: An area controlled by people living in another country. New York was one of the 13 American Colonies controlled by the British.

IMMIGRANT: Someone who comes to a country to live there permanently

INSPECTED: Looked over carefully

RESTORE: To repair something to bring it back to its original condition

REVOLUTIONARY WAR: The war between the American Colonies and the British during 1775–1783. The Colonies wanted to be free from British control.

CULTURE: The beliefs, traditions, art, and language of a group of people at a certain place and time

DEPORTED: Sent back to the country from which a person came

INTERPRETER: A person who puts words in one language into another language

OFFICIAL: A person who is elected or given a specific job, often involving work for the government

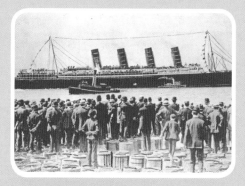

STEAMSHIP: A ship powered by steam engines

STEERAGE: The bottom section of a ship, where passengers paying the cheapest fare traveled

Index

Boldface indicates illustrations.

B
Beame, Abraham 37, **37**
Berlin, Irving 36, **36**

C
Colbert, Claudette 36, **36**
Colonies 14, 46, **46**
Cultures 34, **34–35,** 47, **47**

D
Deportation 19, 21, 25, 28, **28,** 47, **47**

E
Ellis Island
    buildings 16–17, **16–17,** 25, **25**
    cool facts 24–25
    history 12–15, 38, **39**
    hospital 17, **17,** 26, **40**
    main building **4,** 17, **17, 28,**
        42–43
    as museum **42–43,** 43
    Registry Room **22,** 22–23
    restoration **40,** 41, 46, **46**

F
Famous immigrants 36–37, **36–37**
Foxlee, Ludmila Kuchar 31, **31**

H
Health inspections 20–21, **21**
Houdini, Harry 37, **37**

I
Immigrants
    arriving **5, 18**
    beyond Ellis Island 32–33, **32–33**

    definition 5, 46, **46**
    impact 34–37
    origins 11, 25, **25**
Inspections 14, 20–23, **21, 22,** 25, **25,**
    26, 29
Interpreters 22, 24, 29, 47, **47**

J
Johnson, Lyndon 41

L
La Guardia, Fiorello 24, **24**
Lenape Native Americans 12, **13**

M
Map 11
Moore, Annie 4–5, **6,** 7

N
Name changes 29

R
Revolutionary War 14, 46, **46**

S
Statue of Liberty 8, 9, **9**
Steamships 8, 10, **11,** 47, **47**
Steerage 10, **11,** 47, **47**

V
Volunteers 30–31, **30–31**